Great Works **Instructional Guides for Literature**

Bud, Not Buddy

A guide for the novel by Christopher Paul Curtis
Great Works Author: Suzanne Barchers

SHELL EDUCATION

Publishing Credits

Robin Erickson, *Production Director;* Lee Aucoin, *Creative Director;* Timothy J. Bradley, *Illustration Manager;* Emily R. Smith, M.A.Ed., *Editorial Director;* Amber Goff, *Editorial Assistant;* Don Tran, *Production Supervisor;* Corinne Burton, M.A.Ed., *Publisher*

Image Credits

Cover image Africa Rising/Gelpi JM/Shutterstock

Standards

© 2007 Teachers of English to Speakers of Other Languages, Inc. (TESOL)
© 2007 Board of Regents of the University of Wisconsin System. World-Class Instructional Design and Assessment (WIDA).
© Copyright 2010. National Governors Association Center for Best Practices and Council of Chief State School Officers. All rights reserved.

Shell Education

5301 Oceanus Drive
Huntington Beach, CA 92649-1030
http://www.shelleducation.com
ISBN 978-1-4258-8975-3
© 2014 Shell Educational Publishing, Inc.

Table of Contents

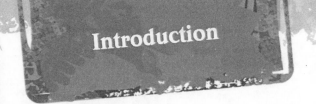

How to Use This Literature Guide

Today's standards demand rigor and relevance in the reading of complex texts. The units in this series guide teachers in a rich and deep exploration of worthwhile works of literature for classroom study. The most rigorous instruction can also be interesting and engaging!

Many current strategies for effective literacy instruction have been incorporated into these instructional guides for literature. Throughout the units, text-dependent questions are used to determine comprehension of the book as well as student interpretation of the vocabulary words. The books chosen for the series are complex and exemplars of carefully crafted works of literature. Close reading is used throughout the units to guide students toward revisiting the text and using textual evidence to respond to prompts orally and in writing. Students must analyze the story elements in multiple assignments for each section of the book. All of these strategies work together to rigorously guide students through their study of literature.

The next few pages will make clear how to use this guide for a purposeful and meaningful literature study. Each section of this guide is set up in the same way to make it easier for you to implement the instruction in your classroom.

Theme Thoughts

The great works of literature used throughout this series have important themes that have been relevant to people for many years. Many of the themes will be discussed during the various sections of this instructional guide. However, it would also benefit students to have independent time to think about the key themes of the novel.

Before students begin reading, have them complete *Pre-Reading Theme Thoughts* (page 13). This graphic organizer will allow students to think about the themes outside the context of the story. They'll have the opportunity to evaluate statements based on important themes and defend their opinions. Be sure to have students keep their papers for comparison to the *Post-Reading Theme Thoughts* (page 64). This graphic organizer is similar to the pre-reading activity. However, this time, students will be answering the questions from the point of view of one of the characters of the novel. They have to think about how the character would feel about each statement and defend their thoughts. To conclude the activity, have students compare what they thought about the themes before the novel to what the characters discovered during the story.

How to Use This Literature Guide (cont.)

Vocabulary

Each teacher overview page has definitions and sentences about how key vocabulary words are used in the section. These words should be introduced and discussed with students. There are two student vocabulary activity pages in each section. On the first page, students are asked to define the ten words chosen by the author of this unit. On the second page in most sections, each student will select at least eight words that he or she finds interesting or difficult. For each section, choose one of these pages for your students to complete. With either assignment, you may want to have students get into pairs to discuss the meanings of the words. Allow students to use reference guides to define the words. Monitor students to make sure the definitions they have found are accurate and relate to how the words are used in the text.

On some of the vocabulary student pages, students are asked to answer text-related questions about the vocabulary words. The following question stems will help you create your own vocabulary questions if you'd like to extend the discussion.

- How does this word describe _____'s character?
- In what ways does this word relate to the problem in this story?
- How does this word help you understand the setting?
- In what ways is this word related to the story's solution?
- Describe how this word supports the novel's theme of . . . .
- What visual images does this word bring to your mind?
- For what reasons might the author have chosen to use this particular word?

At times, more work with the words will help students understand their meanings. The following quick vocabulary activities are a good way to further study the words.

- Have students practice their vocabulary and writing skills by creating sentences and/or paragraphs in which multiple vocabulary words are used correctly and with evidence of understanding.
- Students can play vocabulary concentration. Students make a set of cards with the words and a separate set of cards with the definitions. Then, students lay the cards out on the table and play concentration. The goal of the game is to match vocabulary words with their definitions.
- Students can create word journal entries about the words. Students choose words they think are important and then describe why they think each word is important within the book.

How to Use This Literature Guide *(cont.)*

Analyzing the Literature

After students have read each section, hold small-group or whole-class discussions. Questions are written at two levels of complexity to allow you to decide which questions best meet the needs of your students. The Level 1 questions are typically less abstract than the Level 2 questions. Level 1 is indicated by a square, while Level 2 is indicated by a triangle.

These questions focus on the various story elements, such as character, setting, and plot. Student pages are provided if you want to assign these questions for individual student work before your group discussion. Be sure to add further questions as your students discuss what they've read. For each question, a few key points are provided for your reference as you discuss the novel with students.

Reader Response

In today's classrooms, there are often great readers who are below average writers. So much time and energy is spent in classrooms getting students to read on grade level, that little time is left to focus on writing skills. To help teachers include more writing in their daily literacy instruction, each section of this guide has a literature-based reader response prompt. Each of the three genres of writing is used in the reader responses within this guide: narrative, informative/explanatory, and opinion/argument. Students have a choice between two prompts for each reader response. One response requires students to make connections between the reading and their own lives. The other prompt requires students to determine text-to-text connections or connections within the text.

Close Reading the Literature

Within each section, students are asked to closely reread a short section of text. Since some versions of the novels have different page numbers, the selections are described by chapter and location, along with quotations to guide the readers. After each close reading, there are text-dependent questions to be answered by students.

Encourage students to read each question one at a time and then go back to the text and discover the answer. Work with students to ensure that they use the text to determine their answers rather than making unsupported inferences. Once students have answered the questions, discuss what they discovered. Suggested answers are provided in the answer key.

How to Use This Literature Guide (cont.)

Close Reading the Literature (cont.)

The generic, open-ended stems below can be used to write your own text-dependent questions if you would like to give students more practice.

- Give evidence from the text to support . . . .
- Justify your thinking using text evidence about . . . .
- Find evidence to support your conclusions about . . . .
- What text evidence helps the reader understand . . . ?
- Use the book to tell why _____ happens.
- Based on events in the story, ...
- Use text evidence to describe why . . . .

Making Connections

The activities in this section help students make cross-curricular connections to writing, mathematics, science, social studies, or the fine arts. In some of these lessons, students are asked to use the author as a mentor. The writing in the novel models a skill for them that they can then try to emulate. Students may also be asked to look for examples of language conventions within the novel. Each of these types of activities requires higher-order thinking skills from students.

Creating with the Story Elements

It is important to spend time discussing the common story elements in literature. Understanding the characters, setting, and plot can increase students' comprehension and appreciation of the story. If teachers discuss these elements daily, students will more likely internalize the concepts and look for the elements in their independent reading. Another very important reason for focusing on the story elements is that students will be better writers if they think about how the stories they read are constructed.

Students are given three options for working with the story elements. They are asked to create something related to the characters, setting, or plot of the novel. Students are given choice on this activity so that they can decide to complete the activity that most appeals to them. Different multiple intelligences are used so that the activities are diverse and interesting to all students.

How to Use This Literature Guide (cont.)

Culminating Activity

This open-ended, cross-curricular activity requires higher-order thinking and allows for a creative product. Students will enjoy getting the chance to share what they have discovered through reading the novel. Be sure to allow them enough time to complete the activity at school or home.

Comprehension Assessment

The questions in this section are modeled after current standardized tests to help students analyze what they've read and prepare for tests they may see in their classrooms. The questions are dependent on the text and require critical-thinking skills to answer.

Response to Literature

The final post-reading activity is an essay based on the text that also requires further research by students. This is a great way to extend this book into other curricular areas. A suggested rubric is provided for teacher reference.

Correlation to the Standards

Shell Education is committed to producing educational materials that are research and standards based. In this effort, we have correlated all of our products to the academic standards of all 50 United States, the District of Columbia, the Department of Defense Dependents Schools, and all Canadian provinces.

Purpose and Intent of Standards

Standards are designed to focus instruction and guide adoption of curricula. Standards are statements that describe the criteria necessary for students to meet specific academic goals. They define the knowledge, skills, and content students should acquire at each level. Standards are also used to develop standardized tests to evaluate students' academic progress. Teachers are required to demonstrate how their lessons meet standards. Standards are used in the development of all of our products, so educators can be assured they meet high academic standards.

How To Find Standards Correlations

To print a customized correlation report of this product for your state, visit our website at http://www.shelleducation.com and follow the online directions. If you require assistance in printing correlation reports, please contact Customer Service at 1-877-777-3450.

Correlation to the Standards (cont.)

Standards Correlation Chart

The lessons in this guide were written to support the Common Core College and Career Readiness Anchor Standards. This chart indicates which sections of this guide address the anchor standards.

Common Core College and Career Readiness Anchor Standard	Section
CCSS.ELA-Literacy.CCRA.R.1—Read closely to determine what the text says explicitly and to make logical inferences from it; cite specific textual evidence when writing or speaking to support conclusions drawn from the text.	Close Reading the Literature Sections 1–5; Making Connections Sections 2, 5; Creating with the Story Elements Sections 3, 5; Culminating Activity
CCSS.ELA-Literacy.CCRA.R.2—Determine central ideas or themes of a text and analyze their development; summarize the key supporting details and ideas.	Analyzing the Literature Sections 1–5; Making Connections Sections 2, 5; Creating with the Story Elements Sections 3, 5; Culminating Activity; Post-Reading Response to Literature
CCSS.ELA-Literacy.CCRA.R.3—Analyze how and why individuals, events, or ideas develop and interact over the course of a text.	Analyzing the Literature Sections 1–5; Post-Reading Theme Thoughts; Culminating Activity
CCSS.ELA-Literacy.CCRA.R.4—Interpret words and phrases as they are used in a text, including determining technical, connotative, and figurative meanings, and analyze how specific word choices shape meaning or tone.	Vocabulary Sections 1–5; Making Connections Sections 1, 4; Creating with the Story Elements Sections 2–3, 5; Culminating Activity
CCSS.ELA-Literacy.CCRA.R.5—Analyze the structure of texts, including how specific sentences, paragraphs, and larger portions of the text (e.g., a section, chapter, scene, or stanza) relate to each other and the whole.	Creating with the Story Elements Sections 1–3, 5; Culminating Activity; Post-Reading Response to Literature
CCSS.ELA-Literacy.CCRA.R.10—Read and comprehend complex literary and informational texts independently and proficiently.	Entire Unit
CCSS.ELA-Literacy.CCRA.W.1—Write arguments to support claims in an analysis of substantive topics or texts using valid reasoning and relevant and sufficient evidence.	Reader Response Sections 1–3; Creating with the Story Elements Section 4; Post-Reading Response to Literature
CCSS.ELA-Literacy.CCRA.W.2—Write informative/explanatory texts to examine and convey complex ideas and information clearly and accurately through the effective selection, organization, and analysis of content.	Reader Response Sections 2, 4–5; Creating with the Story Elements Section 4; Post-Reading Theme Thoughts; Post-Reading Response to Literature

Correlation to the Standards *(cont.)*

Standards Correlation Chart *(cont.)*

Common Core College and Career Readiness Anchor Standard	Section
CCSS.ELA-Literacy.CCRA.W.3—Write narratives to develop real or imagined experiences or events using effective technique, well-chosen details and well-structured event sequences.	Reader Response Sections 1, 3–5; Creating with the Story Elements Section 4
CCSS.ELA-Literacy.CCRA.W.4—Produce clear and coherent writing in which the development, organization, and style are appropriate to task, purpose, and audience.	Creating with Story Elements Sections 1, 4; Post-Reading Theme Thoughts; Post-Reading Response to Literature
CCSS.ELA-Literacy.CCRA.W.9—Draw evidence from literary or informational texts to support analysis, reflection, and research.	Close Reading the Literature Sections 1–5; Making Connections Sections 2, 5; Creating with the Story Elements Section 3
CCSS.ELA-Literacy.CCRA.L.1—Demonstrate command of the conventions of standard English grammar and usage when writing or speaking.	Culminating Activity; Post-Reading Theme Thoughts; Post-Reading Response to Literature
CCSS.ELA-Literacy.CCRA.L.4—Determine or clarify the meaning of unknown and multiple-meaning words and phrases by using context clues, analyzing meaningful word parts, and consulting general and specialized reference materials, as appropriate.	Vocabulary Sections 1–5
CCSS.ELA-Literacy.CCRA.L.6—Acquire and use accurately a range of general academic and domain-specific words and phrases sufficient for reading, writing, speaking, and listening at the college and career readiness level; demonstrate independence in gathering vocabulary knowledge when encountering an unknown term important to comprehension or expression.	Vocabulary Sections 1–5

TESOL and WIDA Standards

The lessons in this book promote English language development for English language learners. The following TESOL and WIDA English Language Development Standards are addressed through the activities in this book:

- **Standard 1:** English language learners communicate for social and instructional purposes within the school setting.

- **Standard 2:** English language learners communicate information, ideas and concepts necessary for academic success in the content area of language arts.

About the Author—Christopher Paul Curtis

Christopher Paul Curtis, a native of Flint, Michigan, lives in Detroit, Michigan, with his family. As a young man growing up in Flint, Curtis was eager to earn a living. In his first job at the Fisher Body plant, Curtis hung doors on cars, alternating the task with a coworker. The two young men decided to team up—hanging both sets of doors in 30-minute segments, giving Curtis time to write between turns.

His first book, *The Watsons Go to Birmingham—1963,* was published in 1995. It was a Newbery Honor book and won the Coretta Scott King Award. With the success of this book, Curtis, then in his forties, found he could leave factory work behind and focus on developing a writing career. Curtis draws upon his own experiences and his family in his stories. Two of the characters in *Bud, Not Buddy,* which won the Newbery Medal and the Coretta Scott King Award, were inspired by his grandfathers.

Curtis says that one of the great joys of writing for him is not knowing where the story is going. He thought that *Bud, Not Buddy* would be a story about his grandfather at age ten. Instead, the boy turned out to be an orphan named Bud who went in search of his father.

While Curtis develops a story, he conducts thorough research into the time period and setting. He also revises his work regularly. He says that he enjoys the creative process of writing—sometimes laughing out loud as he works—and he encourages young people to have fun with their writing.

Curtis's works are not limited to paper: *Bud, Not Buddy* and *Mr. Chickee's Funny Money* have both been adapted for the stage. *The Watsons Go to Birmingham—1963* has also been adapted for the stage and was television movie in 2013.

You can read more about Christopher Paul Curtis at his website: http://www.nobodybutcurtis.com.

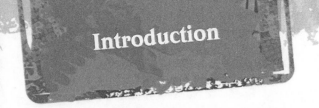

Book Summary of *Bud, Not Buddy*

Bud, age 10, lives in an orphanage during the Great Depression of the 1930s. Sent to a foster home due to overcrowding at the orphanage, Bud finds that the only way to evade abuse is to run away. With his few belongings in a cardboard suitcase, he slips away. At first, he sleeps outside and spends his days in the library. Then, he stays in a Hooverville and tries to ride the rails. Eventually, he sets out on a journey to Grand Rapids, Michigan.

Bud is motivated in his journey by the belief that his father is Herman E. Calloway, a successful musician. Thanks to a kind stranger, he tracks down Calloway's band, discovering that he indeed has a family, although not exactly what he'd anticipated.

The theme of survival runs through *Bud, Not Buddy,* from finding his next meal to the rules he has constructed for "Having a Funner Life and Making a Better Liar Out of Yourself." The setting of the Depression brings to life the desperation faced by many people, all in search of a better life.

Possible Texts for Text Comparisons

There are several other books by the author that can be used to compare his use of setting and history to develop his storylines. *The Watsons Go to Birmingham—1963* follows the Watson family on their journey from Flint, Michigan, to Birmingham, Alabama, after a terrible church bombing. *The Mighty Miss Malone* tells the story of a character who first appears in *Bud, Not Buddy*, as her family struggles with finding work during the Depression. Curtis tackles the issue of slavery in *Elijah of Buxton*, the story of a young boy in the late 1800s who pursues a thief, risking the loss of his freedom.

Cross-Curricular Connection

This book can be used during a social studies unit on the Great Depression or during a literature unit on survival.

Possible Texts for Text Sets

- Hesse, Karen. *Out of the Dust.* Scholastic, 1997.
- Peck, Richard. *A Year Down Yonder.* Puffin, 2002.
- Taylor, Mildred D. *Roll of Thunder, Hear My Cry.* Puffin, 2004.

Name _____

Date _____

Pre-Reading Theme Thoughts

Directions: Read each of the statements in the first column. Decide if you agree or disagree with the statements. Record your opinion by marking an *X* in Agree or Disagree for each statement. Explain your choices in the third column. There are no right or wrong answers.

Statement	Agree	Disagree	Explain Your Answer
It would be great to be on your own.			
People who are poor should just work harder.			
Kids should never trust strangers.			
You can never get over losing someone you love.			

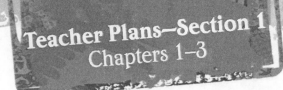
Vocabulary Overview

Ten key words from this section are provided below with definitions and sentences about how the words are used in the book. Choose one of the vocabulary activity sheets (pages 15 or 16) for students to complete as they read this section. Monitor students as they work to ensure the definitions they have found are accurate and relate to the text. Finally, discuss these important vocabulary words with students. If you think these words or other words in the section warrant more time devoted to them, there are suggestions in the introduction for other vocabulary activities (page 5).

Word	Definition	Sentence about Text
depression (ch. 1)	period of low employment	Many people struggle for food and work during the Great **Depression** of the 1930s.
commence (ch. 1)	begin	When Bud's tooth gets loose, it seems like his body might **commence** to fall apart.
engagement (ch. 1)	period of time	A limited **engagement** for a band lasts just a few days.
paradise (ch. 2)	a blissful place	For a liar like Todd, having people always believe you must be **paradise**.
urchin (ch. 2)	brat, rascal	Todd calls Bud a street **urchin**.
tolerate (ch. 2)	allow, put up with	The foster mother, Mrs. Amos, cannot **tolerate** Bud.
ingratitude (ch. 2)	ungrateful	Mrs. Amos doesn't expect **ingratitude** from an orphan.
plague (ch. 2)	upset	Mrs. Amos hopes Bud's guilty conscience **plagues** him after he attacks Todd.
padlock (ch. 2)	lock, bolt	Mr. Amos fastens a **padlock** on the shed door.
revenge (ch. 3)	payback	Bud plans to get his **revenge** on the family.

Name _____

Date _____

Understanding Vocabulary Words

Directions: The following words are in this section of the book. Use context clues and reference materials to determine an accurate definition for each word.

Word	Definition
depression (ch. 1)	
commence (ch. 1)	
engagement (ch. 1)	
paradise (ch. 2)	
urchin (ch. 2)	
tolerate (ch. 2)	
ingratitude (ch. 2)	
plague (ch. 2)	
padlock (ch. 2)	
revenge (ch. 3)	

Name _____

Date _____

During-Reading Vocabulary Activity

Directions: As you read these chapters, record at least eight important words on the lines below. Try to find interesting, difficult, intriguing, special, or funny words. Your words can be long or short. They can be hard or easy to spell. After each word, use context clues in the text and reference materials to define the word.

- _____
- _____
- _____
- _____
- _____
- _____
- _____
- _____
- _____
- _____

Directions: Respond to the questions about these words in this section.

1. Describe how Bud shoots out **apologies** to the Amos family.

_____

_____

2. Will Bud's **conscience** truly plague him about his fight with Todd? Justify your answer.

_____

_____

Analyzing the Literature

Provided below are discussion questions you can use in small groups, with the whole class, or for written assignments. Each question is given at two levels so you can choose the right question for each group of students. Activity sheets with these questions are provided (pages 18–19) if you want students to write their responses. For each question, a few key discussion points are provided for your reference.

Story Element	■ Level 1	▲ Level 2	Key Discussion Points
Plot	How do Bud and Jerry react to the news that they are being moved to foster homes?	Think about how the book begins: *Here we go again.* How does Bud draw on his prior experiences to help Jerry? How does Bud really feel?	Discuss how hard it is to be an older foster child and know that you'll be the underdog and quite possibly bullied. Also discuss the general feeling of helplessness as an orphan.
Character	Why do you think Todd starts the fight with Bud? Who would you choose for a friend?	Contrast Bud's personality with Todd's. How are they alike? Different?	Although Todd is a rather unlikeable character, bring out how Todd might be threatened by having a younger boy in the home. If time allows, explore how Todd manipulates his parents.
Setting	What is it like in the shed?	How does the author make you feel like you are in the shed with Bud?	Discuss the presence of the spider webs, bugs, the fish-head guards, the hornet nest, and the darkness. Contrast the real with the imagined (vampires). If time allows, relate the setting to the set-up by Todd with his description of what previously happened to other kids.
Character	Why is Bud mad at the Amoses *and* at himself?	Bud says that being scared gives you strength. How? He is also angry. Describe how his anger and fear affect his actions.	Bud resents being locked up and for being susceptible to the threat of vampires. The fear gives him strength to get out of the shed. Between the fear and the anger, he is ready to seek his revenge on the Amos family.

Name _____

Date _____

Analyzing the Literature

Directions: Think about the section you have just read. Read each question and state your response with textual evidence.

1. How do Bud and Jerry react to the news that they are being moved to foster homes?

   _____

   _____

   _____

   _____

2. Why do you think Todd starts the fight with Bud? Who would you choose for a friend?

   _____

   _____

   _____

   _____

3. What is it like in the shed?

   _____

   _____

   _____

4. Why is Bud mad at the Amoses and at himself?

   _____

   _____

   _____

   _____

Name _____

Date _____

▲ Analyzing the Literature

Directions: Think about the section you have just read. Read each question and state your response with textual evidence.

1. Think about how the book begins: *Here we go again.* How does Bud draw on his prior experiences to help Jerry? How does Bud really feel?

   _____

   _____

   _____

   _____

2. Contrast Bud's personality with Todd's. How are they alike? Different?

   _____

   _____

   _____

3. How does the author make you feel like you are in the shed with Bud?

   _____

   _____

   _____

   _____

4. Bud says that being scared gives you strength. How? He is also angry. Describe how his anger and fear affect his actions.

   _____

   _____

   _____

   _____

Name

Date

Reader Response

Directions: Choose one of the following prompts about this section to answer. Be sure you include a topic sentence in your response, use textual evidence to support your opinion, and provide a strong conclusion that summarizes your opinion.

Writing Prompts

- **Narrative Piece**—Choose one of the main characters in the book and describe why you would or would not like to be friends with that character.
- **Opinion/Argument Piece**—What advice would you give Bud at this point in the story?

_____

_____

_____

_____

_____

_____

_____

_____

_____

_____

_____

_____

_____

_____

_____

Name _____

Date _____

Close Reading the Literature

Directions: Closely reread the section in the last half of chapter 1, beginning with the paragraph that opens with "The paper was starting to wear out . . ." Continue reading to the end of the chapter. Read each question and then revisit the text to find the evidence that supports your answer.

1. Use the book to describe how Bud keeps the flyers and why they are getting worn out.

   _____

   _____

   _____

   _____

2. According to the paragraph about the picture of him standing with his "giant fiddle," what does Herman E. Calloway look like?

   _____

   _____

   _____

   _____

3. Use the text to identify the characteristics Bud decides his father must have.

   _____

   _____

   _____

4. Bud describes how his mother got upset when looking at a flyer. Do you think that is enough evidence to prove that Herman E. Calloway is Bud's father? Justify your answer based on what you've read in this section.

   _____

   _____

   _____

   _____

Name _____

Date _____

Making Connections–Character Contrast

Directions: Todd and Bud have some likenesses and some differences. Consider each characteristic listed below. Place an *X* under Bud or Todd if you think he shows the characteristic. If both boys show a characteristic, write an *X* under each column. In the final column, include a short reason justifying your answer. For example, you might think that both Bud and Todd are brave because they fight.

Characteristic	Bud	Todd	Your Reasons
brave			
fearful			
smart			
angry			
stubborn			
clever			
adaptable			
kind			
funny			
vengeful			

Name _____

Date _____

Creating with the Story Elements

Directions: Thinking about the story elements of character, setting, and plot in a novel is very important to understanding what is happening and why. Complete **one** of the following activities about what you've read so far. Be creative and have fun!

Characters

Create a character report card for Mrs. Todd. List at least six character traits on it, such as *kindness*. Then, give her a grade for each category. Include a "teacher comment" that explains your reason for each grade.

Setting

Create a diorama or drawing of the shed. Review chapter 3 to include the features of the shed that are particularly frightening to Bud.

Plot

At the end of chapter 3, Bud says that he will get his revenge. List three choices he might make next. Then identify the possible good and bad consequences for each choice. Record your answers in a chart like this on another piece of paper.

Choice	Possible Good Consequence	Possible Bad Consequence

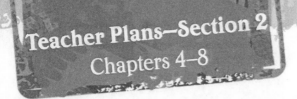
Vocabulary Overview

Ten key words from this section are provided below with definitions and sentences about how the words are used in the book. Choose one of the vocabulary activity sheets (pages 25 or 26) for students to complete as they read this section. Monitor students as they work to ensure the definitions they have found are accurate and relate to the text. Finally, discuss these important vocabulary words with students. If you think these words or other words in the section warrant more time devoted to them, there are suggestions in the introduction for other vocabulary activities (page 5).

Word	Definition	Sentence about Text
lam (ch. 4)	run	Bud has to get away from the Amos family, so he's on the **lam**.
telegraph (ch. 5)	system of sending messages along a wire	**Telegraph** wires, used for communication, were common during the 1930s.
midget (ch. 5)	unusually small	Bud's momma sat on a **midget** horse.
mission (ch. 5)	shelter or place for free food	The **mission** is a place where Bud can get a free breakfast.
crapper (ch. 6)	bathroom (slang)	The man pretends that Bud was in the **crapper** so that he can join them in line.
upside (ch. 6)	upward movement	The man in line hits Bud **upside** the head!
pout (ch. 6)	look annoyed	The kids **pout** because they don't want to share.
retrieve (ch. 7)	reclaim	Bud goes to the desk to **retrieve** his suitcase.
matrimonial (ch. 7)	marriage	Bud is too young to have **matrimonial** plans.
hoodlum (ch. 8)	thug	Bud resents being called a **hoodlum**.

Name _____

Date _____

Understanding Vocabulary Words

Directions: The following words are in this section of the book. Use context clues and reference materials to determine an accurate definition for each word.

Word	Definition
lam (ch. 4)	
telegraph (ch. 5)	
midget (ch. 5)	
mission (ch. 5)	
crapper (ch. 6)	
upside (ch. 6)	
pout (ch. 6)	
retrieve (ch. 7)	
matrimonial (ch. 7)	
hoodlum (ch. 8)	

Name _____

Date _____

During-Reading Vocabulary Activity

Directions: As you read these chapters, record at least eight important words on the lines below. Try to find interesting, difficult, intriguing, special, or funny words. Your words can be long or short. They can be hard or easy to spell. After each word, use context clues in the text and reference materials to define the word.

- _____
- _____
- _____
- _____
- _____
- _____
- _____
- _____
- _____
- _____

Directions: Respond to the questions about these words in this section.

1. In what ways do the Amoses **deserve** what they are getting from Bud?

_____

_____

2. How does Bud look when the librarian says, "There's no need to look so **stricken**"?

_____

_____

Analyzing the Literature

Provided below are discussion questions you can use in small groups, with the whole class, or for written assignments. Each question is given at two levels so you can choose the right question for each group of students. Activity sheets with these questions are provided (pages 28–29) if you want students to write their responses. For each question, a few key discussion points are provided for your reference.

Story Element	■ Level 1	▲ Level 2	Key Discussion Points
Plot	What is it like for Bud to be on the lam?	Describe at least three challenges or dangers that Bud faces while on the lam.	Bud has to find food, a place to sleep, a way to make a living, transportation, etc. If time allows, contrast what he faces compared to what runaways face today.
Character	Describe Bud's momma.	What impact has Bud's momma had on his thinking and ability to respond to challenges?	Discuss the stories that she told and the messages she gave him (when one door closes . . .). She instilled pride in Bud.
Setting	What is it like staying at Hooverville?	Describe the setting at Hooverville and how the people interact with each other.	Discuss shantytowns of the time, which were named Hoovervilles after President Herbert Hoover who was blamed for the economic troubles. Discuss how people pulled together to help each other.
Character	How do you think Bud feels about Deza?	After Bud washes the dishes, Bugs says that Bud looks like he's been "chunked in the head with a rock." What contributes to Bud's appearance?	Bud talks about his life more than he intended, has his hand held by Deza, and has his first kiss. He also learns more about the realities of living without a family.

Name _____

Date _____

Analyzing the Literature

Directions: Think about the section you have just read. Read each question and state your response with textual evidence.

1. What is it like for Bud to be on the lam?

   _____

   _____

   _____

   _____

2. Describe Bud's momma.

   _____

   _____

   _____

   _____

3. What is it like staying at Hooverville?

   _____

   _____

   _____

   _____

4. How do you think Bud feels about Deza?

   _____

   _____

   _____

   _____

Name _____

Date _____

▲ Analyzing the Literature

Directions: Think about the section you have just read. Read each question and state your response with textual evidence.

1. Describe at least three challenges or dangers that Bud faces while on the lam.

_____

_____

_____

_____

2. What impact has Bud's momma had on his thinking and ability to respond to challenges?

_____

_____

_____

_____

3. Describe the setting at Hooverville and how the people interact with each other.

_____

_____

_____

4. After Bud washes the dishes, Bugs says that Bud looks like he's been "chunked in the head with a rock." What contributes to Bud's appearance?

_____

_____

_____

_____

Name _____

Date _____

Reader Response

Directions: Choose one of the following prompts about this section to answer. Be sure you include a topic sentence in your response, use textual evidence to support your opinion, and provide a strong conclusion that summarizes your opinion.

Writing Prompts

- **Informative/Explanatory Piece**—Explain how the book helps you better understand the impact of the Great Depression.
- **Opinion/Argument Piece**—Describe what type of reader would most enjoy the first eight chapters of this book.

_____

_____

_____

_____

_____

_____

_____

_____

_____

_____

_____

_____

_____

_____

_____

_____

_____

Name _____

Date _____

Close Reading the Literature

Directions: Closely reread the section in the middle of chapter 6 about Bud standing in line with his "pretend" family at the mission. Begin with "I stood in line with my pretend family . . . ." Continue reading through six paragraphs. Read each question and then revisit the text to find the evidence that supports your answer.

1. Describe the behavior of the people after they turn the last corner before the mission. Look for descriptive words in the paragraph to support your answer.

   _____

   _____

   _____

   _____

2. Review the paragraph with the description of the gigantic picture. Note the word that the author uses repeatedly in the last two sentences in the paragraph. Explain how the repetition affects the tone of the story.

   _____

   _____

   _____

   _____

3. Find text evidence that shows that the people in the sign must be rich.

   _____

   _____

   _____

   _____

4. Using examples from the text, describe what it looks like inside the building and why it seems worth the wait to Bud.

   _____

   _____

   _____

   _____

Name _____

Date _____

Making Connections—Making Sense of It

Directions: The author, Christopher Paul Curtis, writes his stories so that you are immersed in the plot. You can see, hear, smell, feel, and taste the story. Choose a setting from this section: the library, Hooverville, the river where Bud washes dishes with Deza, the mission, or the train boarding attempt. Write what is happening in the scene using each of your five senses.

Setting	
What I see	
What I taste	
What I smell	
What I feel	
What I hear	

Directions: You might say that the author uses one other sense a lot—the sense of humor. Write an example of when he has made you laugh.

_____

_____

Name _____

Date _____

Creating with the Story Elements

Directions: Thinking about the story elements of character, setting, and plot in a novel is very important to understanding what is happening and why. Complete **one** of the following activities about what you've read so far. Be creative and have fun!

Characters

Think about Bud's personality. Choose four emotions or traits that describe Bud. Write about how each of your choices has a positive and a negative effect on Bud's decisions.

Example: Frightened—Being frightened keeps Bud from taking risks. He may stay safer, but he might also end up missing a chance to find a better life.

Setting

Draw a bird's-eye-view map of Hooverville. Include details such as the location of the huts, shacks, fires, laundry pot, cooking pot, river, train tracks, and trees. Include a map legend (or key), which explains the symbols in the map.

Plot

Recreate this graphic organizer on another sheet of paper to create a circles-of-trouble map for Bud. Think about the problems he's faced since the beginning of the novel. In each circle, write a problem Bud has faced. On each line, record the decision that led to the next problem. One has been done for your reference.

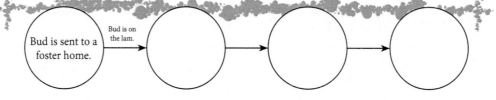

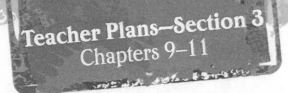
Vocabulary Overview

Ten key words from this section are provided below with definitions and sentences about how the words are used in the book. Choose one of the vocabulary activity sheets (pages 35 or 36) for students to complete as they read this section. Monitor students as they work to ensure the definitions they have found are accurate and relate to the text. Finally, discuss these important vocabulary words with students. If you think these words or other words in the section warrant more time devoted to them, there are suggestions in the introduction for other vocabulary activities (page 5).

Word	Definition	Sentence about Text
pictorial (ch. 9)	with many pictures	The **pictorial** travel book shows many pictures of Michigan.
devour (ch. 9)	gulp, wolf down	Bud **devours** his sandwich in a few bites.
terminally (ch. 9)	incurably	The music group is called **terminally** unhappy.
muffler (ch. 10)	part of a car's system to make it quieter	A noisy old car outside Flint needs a new **muffler**.
definitely (ch. 10)	certainly	Walking alone at night is **definitely** not a good idea.
ventriloquist (ch. 10)	one who can throw his or her voice to entertain	Bud tries to talk like a **ventriloquist**.
bum-rush (ch. 10)	attack	Lefty doesn't try to **bum-rush** Bud.
slew (ch. 11)	a bunch or a lot of something	Adults, like Lefty, often ask kids a **slew** of questions.
backwash (ch. 11)	water or fluid moving backward	Drinking pop while eating may cause **backwash** to collect in the bottle.
knickers (ch. 11)	short pants gathered at the knee	Young boys often wore knee-length **knickers** in the early 1900s.
worrisome (ch. 11)	troublesome	Lefty Lewis has two **worrisome**, but lovable, grandchildren.

Name _____

Date _____

Understanding Vocabulary Words

Directions: The following words are in this section of the book. Use context clues and reference materials to determine an accurate definition for each word.

Word	Definition
pictorial (ch. 9)	
devour (ch. 9)	
terminally (ch. 9)	
muffler (ch. 10)	
definitely (ch. 10)	
ventriloquist (ch. 10)	
bum-rush (ch. 10)	
slew (ch. 11)	
backwash (ch. 11)	
knickers (ch. 11)	
worrisome (ch. 11)	

Name _____

Date _____

During-Reading Vocabulary Activity

Directions: As you read these chapters, record at least eight important words on the lines below. Try to find interesting, difficult, intriguing, special, or funny words. Your words can be long or short. They can be hard or easy to spell. After each word, use context clues in the text and reference materials to define the word.

- _____

- _____

- _____

- _____

- _____

- _____

- _____

- _____

- _____

- _____

Directions: Now, organize your words. Rewrite each of your words on a sticky note. Work as a group to create a bar graph of your words. You should stack any words that are the same on top of one another. Different words appear in different columns. Finally, discuss with your teacher why certain words were chosen more often than other words.

Analyzing the Literature

Provided below are discussion questions you can use in small groups, with the whole class, or for written assignments. Each question is given at two levels so you can choose the right question for each group of students. Activity sheets with these questions are provided (pages 38–39) if you want students to write their responses. For each question, a few key discussion points are provided for your reference.

Story Element	■ Level 1	▲ Level 2	Key Discussion Points
Setting	What is it like outside while Bud walks to Grand Rapids?	Why is Lefty Lewis so uneasy while he is stopped alongside the road to talk with Bud?	Discuss how it is dark, in the middle of the night, full of animal noises, and deserted. Point out the innuendo toward the end of chapter 10 that Owosso isn't a safe place for an African American to be.
Plot	What worries does Bud have after Lefty Lewis stops?	How does Bud's opinion of Lefty Lewis change over time?	Bud thinks at first that Lefty Lewis is a vampire due to the blood in the car. Gradually, his opinion changes, thanks to the food and Lewis's humor and patience. If time allows, discuss the impact of the teasing.
Plot	In chapter 11, Bud talks about his rule for waking up. How does that rule work?	In chapter 11, Bud lists another rule. Discuss how Bud's rules affect his decisions.	Discuss how this particular rule allows Bud to assess the situation, learn a little more about Herman E. Calloway, and plan ahead.
Character	What would it be like to have Lefty Lewis as a father or grandfather?	Describe the relationship between Lefty Lewis and his daughter and grandchildren.	Discuss how Lefty's teasing is tolerated by his daughter and how he encourages his granddaughter to also tease. At the same time, it's loving and delivered with humor. The teasing is not intended to be hurtful.

Name _____

Date _____

Analyzing the Literature

Directions: Think about the section you have just read. Read each question and state your response with textual evidence.

1. What is it like outside while Bud walks to Grand Rapids?

   _____

   _____

   _____

   _____

2. What worries does Bud have after Lefty Lewis stops?

   _____

   _____

   _____

   _____

3. In chapter 11, Bud talks about his rule for waking up. How does that rule work?

   _____

   _____

   _____

   _____

4. What would it be like to have Lefty Lewis as a father or grandfather?

   _____

   _____

   _____

   _____

Name _____

Date _____

▲ Analyzing the Literature

Directions: Think about the section you have just read. Read each question and state your response with textual evidence.

1. Why is Lefty Lewis so uneasy while he is stopped alongside the road to talk with Bud?

_____

_____

_____

_____

2. How does Bud's opinion of Lefty Lewis change over time?

_____

_____

_____

3. In chapter 11, Bud lists another rule. Discuss how Bud's rules affect his decisions.

_____

_____

_____

_____

4. Describe the relationship between Lefty Lewis and his daughter and grandchildren.

_____

_____

_____

_____

Name _____

Date _____

Reader Response

Directions: Choose one of the following prompts about this section to answer. Be sure you include a topic sentence in your response, use textual evidence to support your opinion, and provide a strong conclusion that summarizes your opinion.

Writing Prompts

- **Opinion/Argument Piece**—Bud sets rules about all aspects of his life. Choose one of his rules and relate it to your life and how it might help you.
- **Narrative Piece**—Describe Bud's life if he were to stay with the Sleet family instead of continuing to Grand Rapids.

_____

_____

_____

_____

_____

_____

_____

_____

_____

_____

_____

_____

_____

_____

_____

_____

_____

_____

Name _____

Date _____

Close Reading the Literature

Directions: Closely reread the section toward the end of chapter 11. Begin with the paragraph after the kids say grace. It starts, "Then people started . . . ." Stop reading when Scott and Kim discuss their father, who works as a redcap. Read each question and then revisit the text to find the evidence that supports your answer.

1. Give evidence from the text that describes what two things Bud does before he starts eating and why he does them.

   _____

   _____

   _____

   _____

2. Use text evidence to compare and contrast eating with the Sleets and eating at the Home.

   _____

   _____

   _____

   _____

3. What text helps the reader understand how Bud feels about the meal?

   _____

   _____

   _____

   _____

4. In what ways does the family try to make Bud feel welcome during this scene?

   _____

   _____

   _____

Name _____

Date _____

Making Connections—What Could You Buy with a Nickel?

Lefty Lewis gives Bud a bottle of pop and a sandwich. That bottle of pop cost Lefty a nickel in 1930. That doesn't sound like a lot of money, but people didn't have much money then. Plus, items cost much less at that time.

Directions: The chart shows what you could buy for a nickel in 1930. Find out what each item would cost today. Use advertisements, the Internet, or a visit to the grocery store to find your answers.

Food Item	1930 Price	Today's Price
1 pound of cabbage	3 cents	
1 pound of peas	4 cents	
1 12-ounce bottle of pop	5 cents	
1 pound of spinach	5 cents	
1 loaf of bread	5 cents	
1 can of pork and beans	5 cents	
1 cup of coffee	5 cents	
1 ice cream cone	5 cents	
3 oranges	5 cents	
2 pounds of potatoes	5 cents	

Name_____

Date _____

Chapters 9–11

Creating with the Story Elements

Directions: Thinking about the story elements of character, setting, and plot in a novel is very important to understanding what is happening and why. Complete **one** of the following activities about what you've read so far. Be creative and have fun!

Characters

Christopher Paul Curtis uses a lot of humor in his writing. Think of the characters in Lefty Lewis's family: Lefty Lewis, Kim, Scott, and Mrs. Sleet. Give them a rank on a sense of humor scale, from not funny (1) to very funny (5). Explain why you gave each ranking.

Setting

Recreate a map of Michigan. Mark the route that Bud takes from Flint to Grand Rapids. Indicate the locations for each of the cities mentioned in the book: Flint, Owosso, Ovid, St. Johns, Ionia, Lowell, and Grand Rapids.

Plot

Create a plot excitement graph that compares how exciting each section of the book is so far. The scoring goes from a score of 1 (not very exciting) to 5 (very exciting). Recreate this chart and fill in the boxes to show your reactions. For example, if you think chapters 4–8 are very exciting, shade in the row up to number 5. If it's just average excitement, shade it to number 3. Then tell why you chose each rating.

	1	2	3	4	5	Tell Why
Chapters 1–3						
Chapters 4–8						
Chapters 9–11						

© Shell Education   #40202—Instructional Guide: Bud, Not Buddy   43

Vocabulary Overview

Ten key words from this section are provided below with definitions and sentences about how the words are used in the book. Choose one of the vocabulary activity sheets (pages 45 or 46) for students to complete as they read this section. Monitor students as they work to ensure the definitions they have found are accurate and relate to the text. Finally, discuss these important vocabulary words with students. If you think these words or other words in the section warrant more time devoted to them, there are suggestions in the introduction for other vocabulary activities (page 5).

Word	Definition	Sentence about Text
resourceful (ch. 12)	capable	Bud has to be **resourceful** while on the lam.
alias (ch. 12)	code or secret name	Lefty's name seems more like an **alias** than a real name.
confidential (ch. 12)	private	The plans for the secret union meeting are **confidential**.
premium (ch. 12)	best	The car needs the more expensive **premium** gasoline.
moldering (ch. 12)	decomposing, crumbling	John Brown's decaying bones are **moldering** in a grave.
festering (ch. 13)	rotting	Mr. Calloway is described as having "**festering** nastiness."
meddling (ch. 13)	interfering	It seems like people are always **meddling** with Bud.
stampede (ch. 14)	charge or rush	The hungry band members make a **stampede** to the food.
grouchy (ch. 14)	crabby	Herman E. Calloway seems **grouchy** to Bud.
valve (ch. 14)	controller, such as on a faucet	Bud wishes he had a **valve** to turn off his tears.

Name _____

Date _____

Understanding Vocabulary Words

Directions: The following words are in this section of the book. Use context clues and reference materials to determine an accurate definition for each word.

Word	Definition
resourceful (ch. 12)	
alias (ch. 12)	
confidential (ch. 12)	
premium (ch. 12)	
moldering (ch. 12)	
festering (ch. 13)	
meddling (ch. 13)	
stampede (ch. 14)	
grouchy (ch. 14)	
valve (ch. 14)	

Name _____

Date _____

During-Reading Vocabulary Activity

Directions: As you read these chapters, record at least eight important words on the lines below. Try to find interesting, difficult, intriguing, special, or funny words. Your words can be long or short. They can be hard or easy to spell. After each word, use context clues in the text and reference materials to define the word.

- _____
- _____
- _____
- _____
- _____
- _____
- _____
- _____
- _____
- _____

Directions: Respond to the questions about these words in this section.

1. What does it mean that Bud's momma gave him a good, proper **upbringing**?

   _____
   _____

2. What does it mean to have a dessert that is **on the house**?

   _____
   _____

Analyzing the Literature

Provided below are discussion questions you can use in small groups, with the whole class, or for written assignments. Each question is given at two levels so you can choose the right question for each group of students. Activity sheets with these questions are provided (pages 48–49) if you want students to write their responses. For each question, a few key discussion points are provided for your reference.

Story Element	■ Level 1	▲ Level 2	Key Discussion Points
Plot	Why is Lefty lucky that the policeman didn't find the box of flyers?	What are the labor organizers trying to accomplish in Grand Rapids? Why?	Discuss how Pullman porters and factory workers plan to have a sit-down strike due to poor wages and working conditions. If time allows, compare these efforts to current times. If the flyers had been found, opponents could have used that information to stop the meetings and strike.
Characters	How do the members of the band react to Bud's arrival?	Contrast the band members' reactions to Bud to that of Herman E. Calloway.	The band members ask a lot of questions and tease Bud a lot. Herman E. Calloway states that Bud can't be his son and seems to ignore him from that point on.
Setting	Describe the restaurant and Bud's reactions to it.	How is the restaurant in the story alike and different from restaurants of today?	The restaurant is in a person's home. Like in most of today's restaurants, there are choices, and the food is plentiful. If time allows, discuss how important these experiences were to Bud who rarely had abundant food.
Plot	Why do you think Bud falls apart at the end of chapter 14?	List the factors that lead up to Bud's tears at the end of chapter 14. Why do you think Miss Thomas told him he was "home"?	Bud has run away, has had to deal with a variety of people, and must be exhausted. Miss Thomas probably wants to comfort him and let him know that he is safe.

Name _____

Date _____

Analyzing the Literature

Directions: Think about the section you have just read. Read each question and state your response with textual evidence.

1. Why is Lefty lucky that the policeman didn't find the box of flyers?

_____

_____

_____

_____

2. How do the members of the band react to Bud's arrival?

_____

_____

_____

_____

3. Describe the restaurant and Bud's reactions to it.

_____

_____

_____

_____

4. Why do you think Bud falls apart at the end of chapter 14?

_____

_____

_____

_____

Name _____

Date _____

▲ Analyzing the Literature

Directions: Think about the section you have just read. Read each question and state your response with textual evidence.

1. What are the labor organizers trying to accomplish in Grand Rapids? Why?

_____

_____

_____

_____

2. Contrast the band members' reactions to Bud to that of Herman E. Calloway.

_____

_____

_____

_____

3. How is the restaurant in the story alike and different from restaurants of today?

_____

_____

_____

_____

4. List the factors that lead up to Bud's tears at the end of chapter 14. Why do you think Miss Thomas told him he was "home"?

_____

_____

_____

_____

Name _____

Date _____

Reader Response

Directions: Choose one of the following prompts about this section to answer. Be sure you include a topic sentence in your response, use textual evidence to support your opinion, and provide a strong conclusion that summarizes your opinion.

Writing Prompts

- **Informative/Explanatory Piece**—Describe what real-life people or events you are reminded of by the characters and events in the story.
- **Narrative Piece**—Pick a scene from this section where you think Mr. Calloway handles a situation badly. Rewrite the scene with a more thoughtful Mr. C.

_____

_____

_____

_____

_____

_____

_____

_____

_____

_____

_____

_____

_____

_____

_____

_____

_____

_____

Close Reading the Literature

Directions: Closely reread the section beginning with the first paragraph in chapter 13. Stop reading when Jimmy and Bud shake hands. Read each question and then revisit the text to find the evidence that supports your answer.

1. In the first paragraph, the men in the band are very quiet. Contrast the way the younger men react to Bud's announcement that Herman E. Calloway is his father to how Jimmy and Calloway react.

   _____

   _____

   _____

   _____

2. Reread the paragraph where Calloway says he is sorry about Bud's mom's death. Use text evidence to describe what he thinks of Bud.

   _____

   _____

   _____

   _____

3. What text evidence supports this statement? *Bud thinks that Jimmy is nicer than Calloway.*

   _____

   _____

   _____

   _____

4. How do you know that Calloway and Jimmy do not agree with how to handle Bud's situation?

   _____

   _____

   _____

Name _____

Date _____

Making Connections—What's in a Name?

The band players in the Dusky Devastators have unusual names: The Thug, Doo-Doo Bug, Dirty Deed, Steady Eddie, Mr. Jimmy, and Mr. C.

Directions: Think about why or how they got their nicknames. Create your own band. Have five musicians. Choose a name for the band, the five instruments that they play, and the five members' nicknames. Be creative and have the names connect in some way. For example, if you have a bass drum player she might be called Thumper because she's always thumping her foot to the beat.

My Band Name: _____

Instrument	Nickname	Reason for Name

Name _____

Date _____

Creating with the Story Elements

Directions: Thinking about the story elements of character, setting, and plot in a novel is very important to understanding what is happening and why. Complete **one** of the following activities about what you've read so far. Be creative and have fun!

Characters

Plan an interview as if you are a newspaper reporter. Work with another student. One of you should plan to interview Bud. The other should write interview questions for Herman E. Calloway. Write at least 10 strong questions. Then conduct the interviews with each other. For each interview, have one of you assume the role of reporter and the other one become the interviewee.

Setting

Design a plan for the ideal restaurant. Make a plan that includes a description of the following features:

1. **Appearance** (Describe the room, building, decorations, and so forth.)

2. **Food** (Describe the kind of food, giving examples.)

3. **Service** (Describe how people will be treated and how the food will be served.)

4. **Cost** (Describe the approximate costs of meals. Is your restaurant fancy and expensive or casual and inexpensive?)

Plot

Review the section in chapter 12 about the efforts to begin a union. Make a pro and con chart for the workers as they consider having a strike. Include five reasons for and five reasons against the strike. Think about the rights of the workers, those of the people who use the trains, and those of the employers.

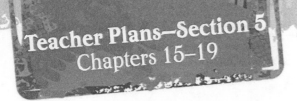

Vocabulary Overview

Ten key words from this section are provided below with definitions and sentences about how the words are used in the book. Choose one of the vocabulary activity sheets (pages 55 or 56) for students to complete as they read this section. Monitor students as they work to ensure the definitions they have found are accurate and relate to the text. Finally, discuss these important vocabulary words with students. If you think these words or other words in the section warrant more time devoted to them, there are suggestions in the introduction for other vocabulary activities (page 5).

Word	Definition	Sentence about Text
nervous (ch. 15)	worried	Bud gets **nervous** at some things the grown-ups say.
contaminated (ch. 16)	dirtied	No one wants to swim in a **contaminated** pool.
particular (ch. 16)	specific	Of the band members, just one **particular** person worries Bud.
copacetic (ch. 16)	satisfactory	Having old things isn't **copacetic** with the band.
carburetor (ch. 16)	part of a car engine	Mr. C. takes apart a **carburetor** to try to fix it.
embouchure (ch. 16)	position of the lips, tongue, and teeth	It takes a while to learn the right **embouchure** for playing a musical instrument.
prodigy (ch. 16)	genius	Bud wants to be a **prodigy** on the saxophone.
offends (ch. 18)	upsets	The teasing never **offends** the band members.
compromise (ch. 18)	negotiate	Mr. Calloway does not **compromise** when it comes to good music.
insinuating (ch. 19)	implying	Miss Thomas asks Mr. Jimmy what he is **insinuating** about Bud.

Name _____

Date _____

Understanding Vocabulary Words

Directions: The following words are in this section of the book. Use context clues and reference materials to determine an accurate definition for each word.

Word	Definition
nervous (ch. 15)	
contaminated (ch. 16)	
particular (ch. 16)	
copacetic (ch. 16)	
carburetor (ch. 16)	
embouchure (ch. 16)	
prodigy (ch. 16)	
offends (ch. 18)	
compromise (ch. 18)	
insinuating (ch. 19)	

Name _____

Date _____

During-Reading Vocabulary Activity

Directions: As you read these chapters, choose five important words from the story. Use these words to complete the word flow chart below. On each arrow, write a word. In each box, explain how the connected pair of words relates to each other. An example for the words *nervous* and *offends* has been done for you.

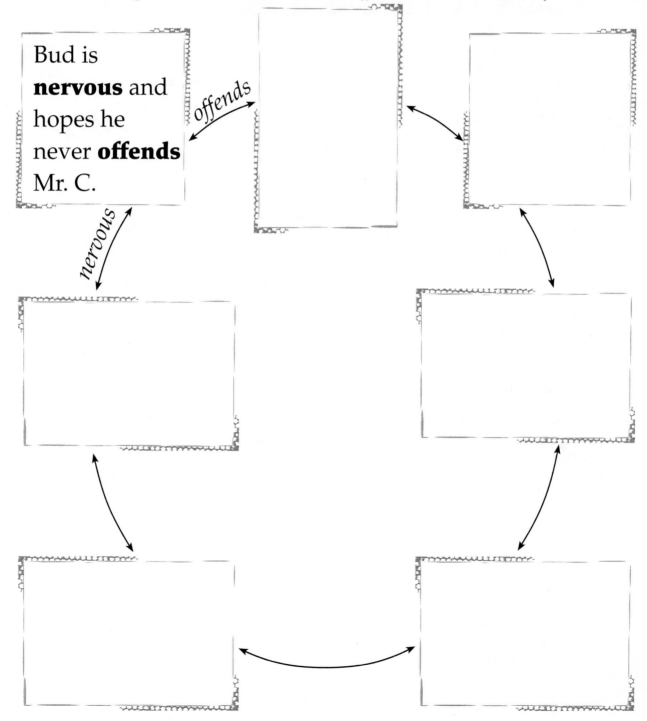

Bud is **nervous** and hopes he never **offends** Mr. C.

offends

nervous

Analyzing the Literature

Provided below are discussion questions you can use in small groups, with the whole class, or for written assignments. Each question is given at two levels so you can choose the right question for each group of students. Activity sheets with these questions are provided (pages 58–59) if you want students to write their responses. For each question, a few key discussion points are provided for your reference.

Story Element	■ Level 1	▲ Level 2	Key Discussion Points
Setting	Why is Bud uncomfortable when he is taken to the bedroom in chapter 15?	Describe how Bud feels about the bedroom he's given in chapter 15. What experiences have probably contributed to his discomfort?	Discuss how Bud has had to sleep in a variety of places, often without family or friends nearby. Bring out how Bud associates the word "gone" with being dead.
Character	Describe the role Miss Thomas plays in having Bud stay with the band.	Why do you think Miss Thomas works so hard at convincing Mr. Calloway to let Bud stay with the band?	Miss Thomas has private discussions with Mr. Calloway, and she is clearly sympathetic toward Bud being an orphan. Bud may have been turned away if she hadn't intervened. She also knows how to work with Mr. Calloway, whose bark may be bigger than his bite.
Plot	What happens in chapter 18 that finally connects Bud to Mr. Calloway?	Describe the role of the rocks in moving the plot along. What else might have happened so that the truth came out?	Mr. Calloway's rock collection provides the link to their connected past. Bud could have gotten his rocks out at another point in the story. He also could have had his mother's picture discovered by another character.
Plot	How does Bud feel about the gift he receives? How important is it?	Describe the significance of the saxophone the band players obtain and repair for Bud.	The band members have chipped in for the saxophone, buying it during the Depression when money is tight. They are nurturing Bud, making him feel a part of the band, with great hopes for the future. Bud, who is not afraid of hard work, is also optimistic about his future.

Name _____

Date _____

Analyzing the Literature

Directions: Think about the section you have just read. Read each question and state your response with textual evidence.

1. Why is Bud uncomfortable when he is taken to the bedroom in chapter 15?

_____

_____

_____

_____

2. Describe the role Miss Thomas plays in having Bud stay with the band.

_____

_____

_____

_____

3. What happens in chapter 18 that finally connects Bud to Mr. Calloway?

_____

_____

_____

_____

4. How does Bud feel about the gift he receives? How important is it?

_____

_____

_____

_____

Name _____

Date _____

▲ Analyzing the Literature

Directions: Think about the section you have just read. Read each question and state your response with textual evidence.

1. Describe how Bud feels about the bedroom he's given in chapter 15. What experiences have probably contributed to his discomfort?

_____

_____

_____

_____

2. Why do you think Miss Thomas works so hard at convincing Mr. Calloway to let Bud stay with the band?

_____

_____

_____

3. Describe the role of the rocks in moving the plot along. What else might have happened so that the truth came out?

_____

_____

_____

_____

4. Describe the significance of the saxophone the band players obtain and repair for Bud.

_____

_____

_____

Name _____

Date _____

Reader Response

Directions: Choose one of the following prompts about this section to answer. Be sure you include a topic sentence in your response, use textual evidence to support your opinion, and provide a strong conclusion that summarizes your opinion.

Writing Prompts

- **Narrative Piece**—Tell about a time in your life when you found a group of people that made you feel very special.
- **Informative/Explanatory Piece**—Choose a member of the band and describe what characteristics you like best about that character.

_____

_____

_____

_____

_____

_____

_____

_____

_____

_____

_____

_____

_____

_____

_____

Name _____

Date _____

Close Reading the Literature

Directions: Closely reread the section towards the beginning of chapter 16 that starts with, "He went outside through a door . . . ." Stop when Bud says, "Yes, ma'am, it's Mr. Calloway." Read each question and then revisit the text to find the evidence that supports your answer.

1. Use text evidence to describe how Bud feels when he wakes up.

    _____

    _____

    _____

2. Use the book to give an example of how the people in Grand Rapids talk. Find at least one example of something that Mr. Jimmy or Miss Thomas says and explain what the saying means.

    _____

    _____

    _____

    _____

3. Use text evidence to tell why Bud feels embarrassed in this section.

    _____

    _____

    _____

    _____

4. Based on the events in the story, why do the band members offer to have Bud stay with them?

    _____

    _____

    _____

    _____

Name _____

Date _____

Making Connections—Effects of the Depression

Directions: Think about the lives of people in the story who are suffering because of the Great Depression. Describe the effects of the Depression on their day-to-day experiences. Draw your information from the story, the Internet, or books. Compare that period in history with today.

	Great Depression	Now
Basic Needs (food, shelter, clothing)		
Jobs and Work Opportunities		
Family Life		
Schooling		

Name _____

Date _____

Creating with the Story Elements

Directions: Thinking about the story elements of character, setting, and plot in a novel is very important to understanding what is happening and why. Complete **one** of the following activities about what you've read so far. Be creative and have fun!

Characters

Choose your least favorite character from the novel. List at least three of his or her personal characteristics (or personality traits) that are based on the actions, statements and thoughts of that character. For each personality trait, describe where in the novel you see evidence of those characteristics.

Setting

Bud is very uncomfortable in the bedroom at first. Create a drawing or diorama that shows the bedroom. Include details from the book.

Plot

Get out your crystal ball and predict Bud's future. Describe what Bud's life might be like in the following years:

- 1941 (age 15)
- 1956 (age 30)
- 1966 (age 40)
- 1986 (age 60)

Name _____

Date _____

Post-Reading Theme Thoughts

Directions: Read each of the statements in the first column. Choose a main character from *Bud, Not Buddy*. Think about that character's point of view. From that character's perspective, decide if the character would agree or disagree with the statements. Record the character's opinion by marking an *X* in Agree or Disagree for each statement. Explain your choices in the third column using text evidence.

Character I Chose: _____

Statement	Agree	Disagree	Explain Your Answer
It would be great to be on your own.			
People who are poor should just work harder.			
Kids should never trust strangers.			
You can never get over losing someone you love.			

Name _____

Date _____

Culminating Activity: Transformations

Directions: Write five main events across the top of the chart. The first column lists contrasting characteristics. Choose one color for each pair of characteristics. (For example, you might choose red for *fearful* and *courageous*.) For each event, think about how Bud acted or reacted during the event. Color in the appropriate box. For example, if Bud was fearful during the first event, color in that section. If he was courageous, color in that section.

	Event 1	Event 2	Event 3	Event 4	Event 5
fearful					
courageous					
weak					
strong					
persistent					
hesitant					
happy					
sad					
hopeful					
pessimistic					

Name _____

Date _____

Culminating Activity: Transformations

Directions: Review your analysis of the events and Bud's reactions. Then choose **one** of the following projects to complete.

- Write a reader's theater script for one event. Make copies and have other students join you to read it aloud to the class.

- Think about the last major event of the story. Write an outline of what you'd like to happen to Bud in a sequel.

- *Bud, Not Buddy* has been turned into a stage play. Create a poster that "sells" people on coming to see the stage version. Be sure that you choose words and images that capture the spirit and times of the story. Base your poster on one of the key events in the book.

Name _____

Date _____

Comprehension Assessment

Directions: Circle the letter for the best response to each question.

1. What does Bud think about for a "funner life"?
    a. the things he did with his mom
    b. a numbered set of rules
    c. things that he did with his friends at the Home
    d. what he might do in the future

2. Why does Bud want to keep control of his suitcase?
    e. He has all his clothes in it.
    f. He keeps money in it.
    g. He keeps souvenirs from his travels in it.
    h. He keeps things that were his mom's in it.

3. Write the main idea of the text below in the graphic organizer.

    "Deed said, 'It's the way of the world, Sleepy. It's against the law for a Negro to own any property out where the Log Cabin is so Mr. C. put it in my name.' Eddie said, 'That, and a lot of times we get gigs playing polkas and waltzes and a lot of these white folks wouldn't hire us if they knew we were a Negro band so Deed goes out and sets up everything.'"

    Main Idea (question 3)

    Details (question 4)   **Details (question 4)**

4. Choose two supporting details from those below to add to the graphic organizer.
    a. African Americans couldn't own property in the 1930s.
    b. White people can be good musicians.
    c. A lot of white people prefer white musicians.
    d. Jazz music was popular in the 1930s.

Comprehension Assessment (cont.)

5. Which statement best expresses a theme of the book?

   a. Music can both soothe and entertain people.

   b. Adults always know what's best for kids.

   c. People were kind during the Great Depression.

   d. It's important to believe in oneself and keep trying.

6. What detail from the book provides the best evidence for your answer to number 5?

   e. "I don't know why, but my eyes don't cry no more."

   f. "From the way the man talked he seemed like he was OK . . . ."

   g. "I could tell those were squeaks and squawks of one door closing and another one opening."

   h. " . . . *singer* wasn't a big enough word to take in the kind of music that was jumping out of Miss Thomas's chest."

7. What is the purpose of these sentences from the book: "'Bud,'" she said, 'Mr. C.—excuse me, your granddad didn't know anything about you. No one knew where your mother had gone.'"

   _____

   _____

   _____

   _____

   _____

   _____

   _____

8. Which other quotation from the story serves a similar purpose?

   a. "This is a hard world, especially for a Negro woman."

   b. "He was so, so proud of that young woman, and he loved her very, very much."

   c. "The more he pushed her, the more she fought him."

   d. "We've been hoping for eleven years that she'd send word or come home, and she finally has."

Name _____

Date _____

Response to Literature: Make Your Case!

Overview: *Bud, Not Buddy* has the Great Depression as the backdrop to the story. Many people, just like Bud, are trying to survive a difficult time period. Here are some facts:

- The stock market crashed in October 1929. President Herbert Hoover had taken office earlier that year. He was blamed for the hardships.

- Shantytowns were named after President Herbert Hoover. Soup eaten by the homeless or poor was called Hoover Stew.

- The biggest hit song of 1932 was "Brother, Can You Spare a Dime?" by Bing Crosby.

- The average income dropped by 40% during the worst years. Many people made about $1,500 per year.

- The Depression got worse in the 1930s. People wanted the federal government to get more involved in the economy. President Hoover refused. He thought people should not get direct help. He believed they'd quit working hard for themselves.

Directions: Think about these questions: Should the government get more involved during tough times? Will it make people lazy if they get handouts or will help give people the encouragement they need to find solutions or work? Write an essay about what *you* think should happen during tough times as described in *Bud, Not Buddy*. Include your views on the role of the government as well as the role of individuals. Also include what you believe organizations, such as soup kitchens, should do.

Your essay response should follow these guidelines:

- State a clear opinion.

- Be at least 750 words in length.

- Include three main points: the role of the government, individuals, and organizations.

- Draw upon, directly or indirectly, the experiences in *Bud, Not Buddy*.

- Provide a conclusion that summarizes your beliefs.

Name _____

Date _____

Response to Literature: Make Your Case!

Directions: Use this rubric to evaluate student responses to *Bud, Not Buddy*.

	Exceptional Writing	Quality Writing	Developing Writing
Focus and Organization	☐ States a clear opinion and elaborates well. Engages the reader from hook through the middle to the conclusion. Demonstrates clear understanding of the intended audience and purpose of the piece.	☐ Provides a clear and consistent opinion. Maintains a clear perspective and supports it through elaborating details. Makes the opinion clear in the opening hook and summarizes well in the conclusion.	☐ Provides an inconsistent point of view. Does not support the topic adequately or misses pertinent information. Provides lack of clarity in the beginning, middle, and conclusion.
Text Evidence	☐ Provides comprehensive and accurate support. Includes relevant and worthwhile text references.	☐ Provides limited support. Provides few supporting text references.	☐ Provides very limited support for the text. Provides no supporting text references.
Written Expression	☐ Uses descriptive and precise language with clarity and intention. Maintains a consistent voice and uses an appropriate tone that supports meaning. Uses multiple sentence types and transitions well between ideas.	☐ Uses a broad vocabulary. Maintains a consistent voice and supports a tone and feelings through language. Varies sentence length and word choices.	☐ Uses a limited and unvaried vocabulary. Provides an inconsistent or weak voice and tone. Provides little to no variation in sentence type and length.
Language Conventions	☐ Capitalizes, punctuates, and spells accurately. Demonstrates complete thoughts within sentences, with accurate subject-verb agreement. Uses paragraphs appropriately and with clear purpose.	☐ Capitalizes, punctuates, and spells accurately. Demonstrates complete thoughts within sentences and appropriate grammar. Paragraphs are properly divided and supported.	☐ Incorrectly capitalizes, punctuates, and spells. Uses fragmented or run-on sentences. Utilizes poor grammar overall. Paragraphs are poorly divided and developed.

#40202—*Instructional Guide: Bud, Not Buddy*   © Shell Education

The responses provided here are just examples of what students may answer. Many accurate responses are possible for the questions throughout this unit.

During-Reading Vocabulary Activity—Section 1: Chapters 1–3 (page 16)

1. Bud announces a series of **apologies** as if he's shooting them out, one after another, to each member of the family.

2. Bud implies that he won't feel bad about his fight with Todd. His **conscience** is clear because Todd started the fight.

Close Reading the Literature—Section 1: Chapters 1–3 (page 21)

1. Bud keeps the flyers in his suitcase. He takes them out to reread them regularly.

2. Calloway looks tired, with a droopy, dreamy look on his face.

3. Bud thinks his father looks quiet, friendly, and smart.

4. Answers will vary. Students should cite text evidence within their answers.

During-Reading Vocabulary Activity—Section 2: Chapters 4–8 (page 26)

1. The Amoses **deserve** what they get because they are so mean to Bud.

2. Bud looks **stricken** because he's upset about the fact that Miss Hill moved away.

Close Reading the Literature—Section 2: Chapters 4–8 (page 31)

1. The people are talking more, like a "bubble busted."

2. Curtis repeatedly uses the word *big*, which underscores the advertisement's message of the white family's importance.

3. They had a big car and all wore "movie star clothes."

4. There are many people, all focused on eating the food.

Close Reading the Literature—Section 3: Chapters 9–11 (page 41)

1. Bud watches what others take to eat and how much the kids put on their forks. Bud wants to make sure he follows what others do so he doesn't look like a pig.

2. The Sleets talk throughout the meal. In the Home, meals were silent.

3. He notices how much the family talks and laughs. They all talk about a variety of topics, such as radio shows, a baseball game, a little girl, and redcaps.

4. Lefty jokes to break the tension at first. Then, they talk to Bud and include him in their conversation. Kim asks her mom to explain what redcaps are. Kim also works to tell Bud about their inside family jokes about Mrs. Sleet's cooking.

Making Connections—Section 3: Chapters 9–11 (page 42)

Listed here are estimated prices to give teachers a reference. These prices will differ based on where you live and what season it is (among other factors).

- 1 pound of cabbage—$2.00
- 1 pound of peas—$3.99
- 1 12-ounce bottle of pop—$1.00
- 1 pound of spinach—$4.50
- 1 loaf of bread—$3.00
- 1 can of pork and beans—$1.00
- 1 cup of coffee—$2.50
- 1 ice cream cone—$2.50
- 3 oranges—$2.25
- 2 pounds of potatoes—$2.00

During-Reading Vocabulary Activity—Section 4: Chapters 12–14 (page 46)

1. Miss Thomas thinks Bud is a polite young man. She credits Bud's momma with raising him right, or giving him a proper **upbringing**.

2. A dessert is free if it is **on the house**.

Close Reading the Literature—Section 4: Chapters 12–14 (page 51)

1. The young men look like they are afraid to laugh. They are quiet. Calloway is disbelieving. Jimmy asks lots of questions.

2. Calloway thinks Bud is a disturbed kid, someone looking for a place to live.

3. Jimmy asks thoughtful questions. He connects Bud to the telegram. He tries to explain that Calloway can't be his father. He thinks someone might be worried about him.

4. Colloway says, "this is your little red wagon, you pull it if you want." In other words, he's saying that Jimmy has to deal with the consequences of keeping Bud around.

Close Reading the Literature—Section 5: Chapters 15–19 (page 61)

1. Bud thinks he has slept like rich people he's seen in movies. He also thinks the two sheets help him sleep.

2. Jimmy asks, "What's the scoop?" That means "What's going on?" He also says "Cop a squat," meaning to sit. Miss Thomas asks if his ears were burning, this is used when a person is being talked about.

3. Bud is embarrassed because Miss Thomas must have undressed him after he fell asleep the night before.

4. They, like Bud and Miss Thomas, think orphanages are "no place to be raised."

Comprehension Assessment (page 67–68)

1. b. a numbered set of rules

2. h. He keeps things that were his mom's in it.

3. Main idea: White men have more privileges than Blacks people do at that time.

4. Supporting Details: a. African Americans couldn't own property then. c. A lot of white people prefer white musicians.

5. d. It's important to believe in oneself and keep trying.

6. g. "I could tell those were squeaks and squawks of one door closing and another one opening."

7. Possible answers include Bud's mother had disappeared or that it wasn't Mr. Calloway's fault that he was confused about Bud and his mother.

8. d. "We've been hoping for eleven years that she'd send word or come home, and she finally has."